Prayers and Litanies for All Occasions

Pray without ceasing – 1Thess 5: 17

Prayers and Litanies for All Occasions

Resource for Christian Living,
Worship and Ceremonies

Eyingbeni Hümtsoe-Nienu

CWI

Christian World Imprints™

First Published in 2017 by

Christian World Imprints(TM)
Christian Publishing & Books from India
H-12 Bali Nagar, **New Delhi-110015**
info@christianworldimprints.com
www.ChristianWorldImprints.com
Phone: +91 11 25465925

ISBN: 978-93-5148-215-4 (HB) ISBN: 978-93-5148-216-1 (PB)

Cataloging in Publication Data--DK
Courtesy: D.K. Agencies (P) Ltd. <docinfo@dkagencies.com>

Hümtsoe-Nienu, Eyingbeni, author.
Prayers and litanies for all occasions : resource for Christian living, worship and ceremonies / Eyingbeni Hümtsoe-Nienu.
pages cm
9789351482154 (HB)
9789351482161 (PB)

1. Prayers. 2. Litanies. 3. Worship programs. 4. Occasional services. I. Title.

BV245.H86 2017 DDC 242.8 23

Printed in India.

To

Mrs (Myrna) Simon Chan

for worshipful life taught and exemplified.

Contents

Foreword

I consider it a great honour to be asked by my former student to write this foreword. All too often, seminary teachers in Northeast India, trying to play catch-up with their peers in other parts of the world, end up disconnected from the church. They no longer feel the living pulse of the faith of grassroots Christians. There is a vast chasm between what they teach in seminary and what they preach in church. Not so Dr Eyingbeni! I am pleasantly surprised to see the same attentiveness to details in this small book of devotions as she does to theological scholarship. In this endeavour she exemplifies what Martin Luther said about the three things that make a theologian: *oratio, meditatio, tentatio* (prayer, meditation, and hardship).

Prayers and Litanies for All Occasions not only touches the significant moments of our lives but the seemingly trivial and mundane routines. They are a poignant reminder that common places can take on new meaning when they are noticed, reflected upon and offered up to—if I may borrow a phrase from the Indian novelist, Arundhati Roy—The God of small things, our heavenly Father who lovingly caresses a fallen sparrow. The use of these elegant prayers goes beyond the occasions for which they are composed; they draw us ineluctably into deep meditation that uplifts the soul.

Some of the prayers could be used for personal "occasional meditation" ("Shopping"); others set in the litany format, for special public events for which Nagas seem to have a particular fondness, such as "House Warming" and "Family Sunday"; still others ("Confession" and "Thanksgiving") could be used to great profit during a regular Sunday worship. Its size and content makes it a suitable *vade mecum* for laypersons, pastors and theological educators who are constantly on the move. It justly deserves wide circulation.

Simon Chan, PhD
Trinity Theological College
Singapore

Preface and Acknowledgments

Prayer as communication with God can occur at any time, place, and circumstance. But there are times when words fail us and we deem it OK not to pray at all. The question of, "How to pray?" is as valid as, "When to pray?" There is no specific way of praying or a particular place for praying because prayer can be said every time and everywhere. God fills the universe and thus is constantly accessible. The prayers herein are a reflection of that theological belief. They are primarily aimed at guiding readers to find meaning for themselves in the words expressed. The readers may combine one or more prayer lines to fulfill their required expectations for any event. Prayers from one section may be adapted to suit another occasion and so also the arrangements, which can be altered to fit in to a particular need.

Although absolutions are strictly not prayers, yet it has been included to convey the message of God's gracious response to human's prayer. All absolutions herein are extracted from the Bible believing that only God has the last word on the conditions of human sinfulness. All other prayers are original to the author. They're inspirations received in worship, at home, on streets, during quiet reflections, by nature, global and local events, technology and everyday whereabouts.

I want to thank some special people behind this book. I'm much grateful to Rev. Dr Simon Chan for taking the time to write the foreword. My admiration for him as an acclaimed scholar, dedicated teacher, committed servant of God, an honorable person with a heart bigger than his name, is bolstered by his gesture of humility in gracefully agreeing to be a part of this modest project.

I cannot forget his wife, Mrs (Myrna) Chan, for her liturgical influence in my life. Much of what I've come to appreciate concerning meaningful worship and heartfelt prayers have been aroused in me by her teachings, exhortations, and practical exposure to several worship traditions through involvement in her ministry – *Global Praise Team* (Singapore). Her contagious passion for worship, worthy of the Sovereign God, has impacted this literary venture in a manner she herself may not have anticipated. To her, with sincere appreciation, I joyfully dedicate this book.

To Sudhanshu Kanda of Christian World Imprints, for his persuasive yet gentle reminders relating to the publication of this book. At times, his kind of push is just what makes it possible to complete a project! To the blurb writers – Dr Vee, Loliro and Chin Yee, my sincere appreciation for your invaluable opinions. Mr Zhalie, my husband, for his proof reading acumen coupled with his enthusiasm and support in seeing through the completion of this book, "thank you".

Eyingbeni Hümtsoe-Nienu

INVOCATIONS

God of the universe,
Fill this place with your presence,
Till we are full with your Spirit,
And we ourselves are not apart from you.
In Christ's name we ask.
Amen.

****

Holy God,
Take away from us desires to be entertained,
And replace them with a longing to meet you;
Remove all hindrances within and without us,
And restore the faith of your Son Jesus Christ in us,
That our worship may be pleasing to you and worthy of your name.
Amen.

****

Lord God,
In the quietness of the hour,
Let only your voice be heard.

In the worship due to you,
Let our submission be no less than whole.
Amen.

****

Lord over all things,
Take control over our thoughts and desires,
That all may come under your command;
That we may render a worship truly worthy of your Sovereignty.
In Jesus' name, Amen.

****

Descend upon us, God Almighty,
And be glorified in our devotion.
Make the songs we sing, the Scripture we read, the Word spoken and heard, prayers lifted to you,
And gifts offered,
Bring you honor and glory as befits our Lord Eternal.
Amen.

****

All knowing God,
We bring to your throne our fears and doubts, our pride and self-centeredness;
That before your majesty we may forget our frailties and worship you for your own name's sake.
Amen.

****

Love divine,
By your grace in Jesus Christ,
Let your visitation in our midst bring hope to the despairing,
Freedom to those bound by powers and principalities,
Solace to the restless,
And glory to your name. Amen.

****

O Holy Spirit,
Breathe on us and revive our spirits,
That in the clarity of our minds,
We may offer perfect worship,
To the honor of your name alone.
Amen.

****

Come, Holy Spirit, like on the day of Pentecost,
Come like the rush of a violent wind,
Fill this entire place.

Unite us,
Though of different tongues, color, tribe and nation,
Rest on us and help us speak your works of power.
To the glory of our Creator, Redeemer and Enabler.
Amen.

(Cf., Acts 2: 1-11)

****

CONFESSIONS

ONE: Gracious God,
I'm like a withered leaf:
Dry and lifeless from all the habits of sin.
Forgive me,
And like the wind that blows away dead leaves,
Making way for new shoots unto fruition,
Let your Spirit clean out all that forbids me
From growing and bearing fruit,
In Jesus' name.
ALL: Amen

◇

ONE: Search me Oh God,
And find my heart today;
Click on me Oh Lord,
And view my thoughts today;
Check if there be any errors in me,
Delete or redo my every sin,
And save me.
ALL: Amen.

(Adapted from Ps 139:23-4)

◇

ONE: Holy God,
Awesome is your presence,
Dreadful is the absence of holiness within me;
Woe to my unclean heart,
Lips and mind;
Touch me with the coal of your Spirit
That my guilt may depart from me,
And my sin be blotted out.
ALL: Amen.

(Adapted from Is 6: 5-7)

◇

ONE: We are a generation of unholy people,
ALL: Forgive us.

ONE: We have wandered far from your ways,
ALL: Forgive us.

ONE: We have forgotten to love our neighbors,
ALL: Forgive us.

ONE: WE have forsaken the widows and the orphans,
ALL: Forgive us.

ONE: We have rejected the sad and the lonely,
ALL: Forgive us.

ONE: We have despised the poor and the weak,
ALL: Forgive us.

ONE: We are sorry for our failures and we pray for your grace and compassion to indwell us and enable us to live as children worthy of the name of Jesus, the Savior of the world.

ALL: Amen.

◇

ONE: God of the land,

ALL: Forgive human excesses in plundering and ravaging your earth.

ONE: God of the ocean,

ALL: Forgive human wrong in poisoning the waters and life therein.

ONE: God of the sky,

ALL: Forgive human apathy in polluting the air and destroying our eco-sphere.

ONE: God of justice,

ALL: Forgive human greed in accumulating more than is needed and leaving others with nothing.

ONE: God of the Universe,

ALL: Forgive human pride to Lord it over your creation.

ONE: God of mercy,

ALL: Forgive human for without your forgiveness we would be reduced to ashes without hope.

ONE: In Jesus' name,
ALL: Amen.

◇

Gracious God,
Forgive us for we have spoken lies against our neighbors,
We have coveted their properties,
We have wished adversity for them,
And rejoiced at their hardship.

We repent of our shameful ways and pray your Spirit to help us become neighbors like the "Good Samaritan" approved by you for your name's sake. Amen.

(Cf. Lk 10: 25-37)

◇

ABSOLUTIONS

Absolutions

I

ONE: If anyone is in Christ, there is a new creation
Look! Everything old has passed away,
Everything new has become new
ALL: All this is from God. Praise be to him!

(2Cor 5: 17; Is 42: 9)

II

ONE: Hear! The Lord who made you,
And formed you in the womb is your redeemer.
He has swept away your transgressions like a cloud;
And your sins like mist.
ALL: Glory be to God. Amen.

(Is 44: 1-2, 22)

III

ONE: Hear, Oh people of God
Your sun shall no more go down,
Or your moon withdraw itself;
For the Lord will be your everlasting light,
And your days of mourning shall be ended.
ALL: Amen.

(Is 60: 20)

IV

ONE: Hear the Word of the Lord!
Because you have returned to me,
I will comfort you as a mother comforts her child.

ALL: We believe and our hearts rejoice. Amen.

(Is 66: 13-14)

V

ONE: The testimony of the Prophet is sure that the seraph touched his mouth with the burning coal and said, "Now that this has touched your lips, your guilt has departed and your sin is blotted out." Likewise, God through the Holy Spirit has forgiven and sanctifies you daily.

ALL: Holy is the Lord of hosts. Glory be to him.
Amen.

(Is 6: 7; 3)

VI

ONE: Since you have humbled yourselves, sought the face of God and turned from your wicked ways, The Lord heard from heaven and forgave your sins and healed your land

ALL: The name of the Lord be praised. Amen.

(2Chro 7: 14)

VII

ONE: The Lord is a gracious God and merciful,
Slow to anger, abounding in steadfast love,
And ready to relent from punishing

ALL: Praise be to God who hears our cries and forgives us

(Jon 4: 2; 3: 8-10)

VIII

ONE: God pardons iniquity and passes over transgressions
He does not retain his anger forever because he delights in showing mercy. He has again compassion on you and trod your iniquities under his foot
And cast all your sins into the depths of the sea.

ALL: Amen

(Mic 7: 18 & 19)

IX

ONE: Happy are those whose transgressions are forgiven, whose sin is covered

ALL: Happy are those to whom the Lord imputes no iniquity. Amen

(Ps 32: 1-2)

X

ONE: I acknowledge my sin to you and I did not hide my iniquity;
I confessed my transgressions to you

ALL: And you forgave the guilt of my sin: I will be glad and rejoice in the Lord. Amen.

(Ps 32: 5, 10)

XI

ONE: If we confess our sins he who is faithful and just will forgive us our sins and cleanse us from all unrighteousness

ALL: Let your word dwell in us. Amen

(1Jn 1: 9, 10)

XII

ONE: Jesus Christ, the faithful witness, the firstborn of the dead, and the ruler of the kings of the earth loves us, and frees us from our sin by his blood

ALL: To him be glory and dominion forever and ever. Amen

(Rev 1: 5b, 6)

THANKSGIVING

Season's Gratitude

Summertime Respite

The sun that peeps through the trees,
Bringing the warmth of the dawn.

The clouds that pass over the sky,
Proving a shade over heated heads.

The shower of rain on earth,
Calming the restless who moan.

At the descend of the sun beyond the horizon,
The heat says goodbye.

The breeze makes its way in;
And the moon gently makes its entrance.

Thanks be to him,
For he gave us well.
Amen

Monsoon Rhapsody

Rhythmic rain,
In your sound and movement,
We hear the footsteps of the rain Maker;
In your downpour,
Children's laughter and joyful glee harmonize;
In your outpouring,
The homemakers and the well-diggers rejoice;
In your timely visit,
The crops and paddy fields see divine favor;
In your constant rhythm,
The oceans, rivers and springs find life.
As you flow,
So does our praise to you Oh Lord. Amen.

◇

Spring Blossoms

Springing from plants, trees and vines,
Flowers, leaves and fruits of all kinds;
A fresh leaf here and a bud there,
Sprouting baby cucumbers and corns bring cheer.

Late in the season,
They all will bloom and yield fruit;
Smiles radiant on the cheek of roses and dahlias,
Even a cactus blushes with health!

The birds hasten their flight,
The bees buzz and dance merrily;
Soft gentle rays from above match -
The fluttering of the butterflies.

The season that heralds regenerated life,
Is surely a symbol of Christ,
Who makes all things new!
Blessed be his name.
Amen.

◇

Winter Yuletide

What does winter bring for me, a Christian?
Pork, cakes and cookies that make me swell?

Does it bring me gifts, stars and lights?
Or takes me to endless buying and senseless bargaining?

I love the carols and the nativity scenes,
Relish the Christmas trees and the colors red, silver, gold and green.

Friends and family around the fire,
Telling jokes and bursting into peals of laughter,
Scaring sorrows away.

Popcorns and finger wafers crackling on the stove,
Music bursting in a distant hill.

It's surely a season of them all;
And winter would feel much colder without them.
But that's not why I wait for winter.
I wait for you because you bring to memory the birth of the Savior.

Even if all yuletide pleasures were to be missing,
Winter would still be a favorite of the seasons.
It brings with it a message of the end of sin and death;
As well points to the beginning of a new life in the Christmas child.

What then should winter bring you for the world, Oh Christians?
Forgiveness unlimited, grace undeserving and love unconditional.

And how should I react to these that Christ brings?
Receive them with a grateful heart and live knowing one's unworthiness of the gifts.

If I but could live up to the blessings of the winter,
I would simply remember the love of Christ my Lord and be content with nothing else.

And if I could send a birthday present to him,
I would wrap my heart filled with praises, for that truly is all he ever wants.
To his eternal glory. Amen.

Thanksgiving in Trials

ONE: Gracious God,
The day is far from over,
The hurts are least healed;
ALL: Yet I will thank you.
ONE: Those that seek to harm me are powerful,
I'm weak and my voice is unheard;
ALL: Yet I will thank you.
ONE: The arms of the powerful are strong and long,
As for mine, they can only fold and pray;
ALL: Yet I will thank you.
ONE: The words of those who wish to crush me are as salt to wounds,
They burn me from inside;
ALL: Yet I will thank you.
ONE: The feet of the oppressors are quick to trample,
Mine are enfeebled by a broken spirit;
ALL: Yet I will thank you.
ONE: The day hangs on like scorching sun,
The night will be just as biting;
ALL: Yet I will thank you.
ONE: The balm of Gilead will surely heal,
Wholeness shall crown me;
ALL: And I will thank you.
ONE: The stars and the moon shall be a delight,
The day shall be as joyous as the night;
ALL: And I will thank you.
ONE: The falsehood of devourers shall be shut as you did

the mouths of the lions in the den with Daniel,
Those who seek to live by their own might shall be brought low;

ALL: And I will thank you.

ONE: Prideful people will see your might,
They shall turn from their wickedness and you will pardon;

ALL: And I will thank you.

ONE: Help me learn to remain thankful,
And humbly submit to your wisdom;

ALL: Amen.

(Cf., I Thess 4:17)

◇

Thanksgiving for Family

1

God,
Thank you for my family.
My mother, who birth and nurtured me;
My father, who took me places;
My sister/s, who locks away my secrets;
My brother/s, who promptly jumps to my rescue;
My grandpa, who prays for unceasingly;
My grandma, who takes time to tell me stories.
Thank you for each of them;
Life is much better with them all!
Amen.

2

My heavenly parent,
I am the only child,
I have my father and my mother,
But thank you for making Jesus my brother,
And the Holy Spirit my sister dear.
Amen.

3

Thank you God,
For our daughter/s, lovely to behold;
Our son/s, charming in stature.
Grant them your wisdom;
That their loveliness and charm,
be to you a constant fragrant offering.
In Jesus, Amen.

4

The tiny baby in my arms,
Is a reminder,
Lord,
Of your motherhood.
The bawling girl/boy in my arms, picked from the ground,
Is a reflection,
Lord,
Of your fatherhood.
The people hand in hand,

Is an image,
Lord,
Of your friendship.
Thank you for being my all.
Amen.

5

When parents are far away,
Siblings nowhere in sight,
You send a neighbor my way,
To tell me you are the one who knows and meets all our needs.
Thanks be to God.
Amen.

◇

God in every Season

ONE

It's wintertime!
My life has come to a standstill,
As though frozen in time under heavy snow;
I'm unproductive.
But your Spirit's warmth is thawing me up,
And you'll soon help me to be fruitful.

ALL

Thanks be to God.

ONE

It's springtime!

All the pretty blossoms cannot lighten the heaviness inside;

Like a pretty flower without fragrance am I;

I'm lonely.

But your Son's grace beckons me come,

To freely receive his rest and peace.

ALL

Thanks be to God.

ONE

It's summertime!

My spirit plays see-saw,

Like the sudden switch between sunshine and rainfall;

I'm unstable.

but your constant love surrounds me,

And it'll lift my lows and fill my highs.

ALL

Thanks be to God.

ONE

It's autumn/fall!

The broken pieces in me are falling apart,

Like the leaves on the tree blown hither and thither by rough winds;

I'm damaged.

But the Cross can mend me,

And put the pieces together and make me whole again.

ALL

Thanks be to God. Amen

◇

Glorious Food

Chilli, tomatoes, ginger,
From gardens in the backyard;
Veggies to cleanse.

Pork, chicken, beef,
From farms near and far;
Meat to strengthen.

Orange, kiwi, guava,
From orchards at home and abroad;
Fruits to nourish.

Rice, wheat, corn,
From fields in a distance;
Staples to energize.

Cloves, cinnamon, fennel,
From tress in unknown forests;
Spices to flavor.

Farmers planted,
Traders delivered,
But God caused them to grow;
All glory be to you.
Amen.

WORSHIP SERVICES

Born is the Savior

Bethlehem's Child,
You were born to be a Savior.
Look on us with pity,
For we are still as sinful as when you found us.

Bethlehem's Child,
Be born in our lives, our homes and our nations.
Look on us with favor,
For we continually desire to be as sinless as how you make us.

Bethlehem's Child,
Be ever born.
Till we see you in glory,
For that is what you come every moment to give us.
Amen.

The Light is Come

ONE: Light of the world,
ALL: Dispel the darkness around it,
Show us by your light,
Its filth,
Its unworthiness -
Before your holiness.

ONE: Light of all Lives,
ALL: Warm the coldness inside us,
Enliven us by your light,
Grant us joy,
And peace -
Beside your presence.

ONE: Light of Salvation,
ALL: Lead creation to your grace,
Direct us by your light,
To confess,
And repent,
Beneath your cross.

ONE: Light of Eternity,
ALL: Guide us to the way of life,
Restore us by your light,
To seek truth,
Love charity -
Being ever near you.
Amen.

******

The Christmas Gifts

In darkness you came as light,
In despair you are hope,
In sin you are salvation.

To those who seek you, may they be found,
To those who fear, may they be consoled,
To those ashamed, may they be forgiven.

Cause the heart to celebrate with joy,
The soul to mourn for renewal,
The flesh to repent from evil.

Turn us from ourselves to you,
Your people,
Your church,
Your world.

That your seed of love sent in Jesus
would grow within us,
and from us to all unto eternity.
Amen.

******

Christmas Intercession

God of love,
Visit your world today,
And let the Savior be born yet again.

See the evils of today,
Your children have forsaken your name and ran after idols of their own creation;
They have exchanged you for money, fame, and evil pleasures.

See the Herods of the day,
They claim to want to worship you but their motives are far from it;
They annihilate innocent children, and helpless, poor folks for selfish gains.

See the Sadducees and Pharisees of our time,
They abuse your name, your message and worship place;
Your holy name skips their tongue, the Gospel is forgotten and your Church is a business center.

See the self-righteous bigots in our world now,
They are quick to condemn and painfully slow to show mercy;
In the guise of religion and tradition, communities are divided, families broken, individuals shunned.

We weep for your world as did Rachel for her children,
Send your Son back to us,
To live and walk among your people in the Holy Spirit;
And let the sick be healed, the guilty pardoned, women and children be dignified, Gentiles and Jews be restored and the Devil be shoved behind.

To the glory of your name.
Amen.

(Cf., Jer 31: 15)

******

Bethlehem's Hope

Bethlehem,
Blessed are you among all cities on earth;
God picked you to be born in.
It was not your beauty or riches,
for you had none in abundance.
It was not your past or present,
For you had nothing to boast about.
He simply chose you for a future bestowed with glory unimaginable.

And so he picks up his children,
Despite all their hidden filth and open weaknesses;
Their broken past and damaged present;
To be born in them,
To give them abundant life and a future.

As Bethlehem opened its gates and its inn for the birth of the Savior,
So must we, whose hearts are closed, shamed and full of self.

Jesus only seeks a place to be born in,
He asks no other fancy room except your very own self,
He cares not the state of it;
For only he can turn a stable into a royal throne.
Blessed be his name. Amen.

****

Children's Nativity Prayers

I

Dear God,
During Christmas help me remember that,
Santa is not my Savior,
Only Jesus is.

And help me to share my gifts,
Just as you gave your life for me.
Amen.

II

Lord Jesus,
Thank you for coming to earth,
For holding us in your arms,
and dandling us on your laps.
When big people pushed us away,
You drew us close to you,
Making us the center of your message.
Thank you for showing such great love to us.
Amen.

III

Our God in heaven,
I am a little girl/boy,
My hands are so small,
My pockets are empty,
I cannot buy Jesus anything.
But my heart is pure;
Take it and make it your favorite gift.
Amen.

IV

Dear Jesus,
Come into my heart,
And be born again.
Make it your home,
And grow in me.
Let it be yours,
For all eternity.
Amen.

V

Dear Jesus,
From heaven you came,
To show me your love.
From earth I come,
To give you my heart.
Make all that is of earth,
Fit for your heavenly glory.
Amen.

****

Maundy Thursday

Lord,
We bring our feet at your holy presence,
Waiting to be washed of all that crucifies you
over and over again.
Amen.

xxxxxxxx

Jesus,
Grant to us a heart to serve,
And like the woman with alabaster jar of costly
nard,
Break ourselves before you
And render to you good service
As befits a Savior.
Amen.

(Cf., Mk 14: 3-9)

xxxxxxxx

Love divine,
Who taught us to love one another,
With a love with which you have loved us,
Grow in us and aid us to yield fruits of love,
That the world may know we are your own.

To the glory of the Triune God.
Amen.

(Cf., Jn 13: 34-35)

xxxxxxxx

Jesus our Lord and Teacher,
Unworthy as we are,
We desire for you to wash our heads, hands and feet.
And so cleansed,
Our pride will leave us,
To nobly serve you,
By joyful washing of every feet,
That is of any gender, class, caste, race, ethnicity and faith.
Amen.

(Cf., Jn 13: 1-15)

Good Friday

Good Friday Lamentation

My Savior!

They hurled abuses at you,

Spit, flogged and loaded your shoulder with a heavy cross.

They pierced your sides,

Fed you sour drink, mocked and tore your clothes and cast lot to divide it.

They mocked your divinity,

And questioned your ability to save.

We do the same to you today -

Wherever there is insult of the poor,

Discrimination and oppression of the marginals.

Wherever there is exclusion of women, children and disabled.

Wherever humans rather obey the Devil than follow your examples.

Woe are we!

For we have failed to live up to your name.

We have neither loved "others",

Nor counted them as equals.

We have forgotten your Lordship and trusted in earthly powers.

Forgive us yet again!

We might not have known what we were doing.

Make us realize that you are God became vulnerable at the hands of cruel men.

Rebuke the voices of doubt inside us and let us hear you say: "Truly I say to you, today you will be with me in Paradise."

Amen.

(Cf., Lk 23: 1-43)

+++++++

Joseph's Litany

ONE: My God the Messiah who has come to establish peace for peoples and for everything on land, sea, and sky.

ALL: Blessed be the God of Joseph.

ONE: From a Jewish town of Arimathea I came to behold your face. You made me believe in you, the long expected Savior. Only you can put such faith in me.

ALL: Blessed be the God of Joseph.

ONE: The unbelief of the supposedly righteous leaders put you on the cross. They recognized not your authority or you as the one who fulfills the law.

ALL: Blessed be the God of Joseph.

ONE: The Council of elders, chief priests and scribes questioned your deity and mocked your kingship. They accused you of perverting the people by your teachings. Your grace has prevented me from being party to such lies.

ALL: Blessed be the God of Joseph.

ONE: It was a privilege to take you from Pilate and give it final respect. From out of many, you have chosen me to clothe and entomb your body.

ALL: Blessed be the God of Joseph. May his name live forever. Amen.

(Cf., Lk 23: 50-53)

+++++++

Easter

Lord of life,
Blessed be to your name for conquering death.
Now we live in hope knowing that like you,
We too shall rise to live with you forever.
Amen.

+++++++

Resurrected Savior,
On Easter morning we are reminded that
there is no other God but you.

You proved your divinity by defeating death
– the final power that separates you from
created beings.

Thank you that your resurrection continues
to be our foundation of hope for new life here
and now and in eternity.

+++++++

Living God,

Bring forth life into all that seems dead in our communities and churches:

Bring an end to corruption of all sorts that kills the spirit of living;

Squash the plans of the powers-that-be that morally and actually assassinate truth and justice seekers;

Purge the minds and hearts that seek to slay the message of love, peace and righteousness - your kingdom values, for worldly ends;

Revive your people in the power of your Holy Spirit that your disciples may faithfully follow the ways of their master and teacher, our Lord Jesus Christ;

And may Easter be real everyday till he returns in glory and our lives become like his forever. Amen.

+++++++

Missions

Minister: Lord, as you send your servant out into the world, look on her with mercy – She is like a lone sheep among many wolves;

People: Protect her Almighty God.

Minister: In times of trials, when wolves seem to beckon her to leave and run away from your fold, go ahead of her and provide your staff of courage to drive evil powers away;

People: Defend her Almighty God.

Minister: As she traverses the wilderness in search of other wandering sheep to bring to your fold, guide her steps through rough and rugged terrain;

People: Lead her Almighty God.

Minister: In Christ our true Shepherd's name we pray.
All: Amen.

~~~~~~~
~~~~~~~

Missionary's Prayer

God, from the beginning of time you have been a sending God.

You sent your Spirit to the world to do your work of liberating people from slavery and injustices.

You sent kings and prophets to dispense truth and speak your message of righteousness.

You sent nature and common people to convey your judgment.

Ultimately you sent your only Son Jesus Christ to reveal yourself and your ways to creation.

Send me out today to continue the task that those whom you sent ahead have started.

Clothe me with humility to accept that I have no message except you.

Let your wisdom instruct me to build nothing else but your kingdom.

In your love, may I be fully soaked to understand that my best sacrifices pale in comparison to what Christ has done in love.

Amen

~~~~~~~
~~~~~~~

Church Ministry

ONE

The harvest is plentiful, O God of the universe. And we joyfully send more laborers into your field; that there will be feasting in your house in eternity.

Prepare the harvesters with all the needed tools and knowledge to bring in harvest to the fullest extent; that none will be left out from joining the heavenly banquet.

Endow the workers with diligence and passion to labor on till the task is done; that they themselves may not be denied entry into the joy of the master.

ENTRANT

So help me, O God of universe, to do your bidding to the praise and glory of your name.

ONE

May the blessing of the triune God be with you.

ALL

Amen.

~~~~~~~
~~~~~~~

Entrants

Tasks may vary,

Places may change,

People and cultures may differ,

But Lord, we are at your service.

Whatever you make us do,

Wherever you take us,

Whoever we live amongst,

We gladly yield to your plan.

Only grant us strength to bear all weights,

Endurance to journey anywhere,

Patience for harmonious coexistence,

Faith to trust in your wisdom.

In weakness of spirit,

Sickness of body,

Perplexity of reality,

Embrace us completely till your grace renews our being.

In the name of Jesus, who called us to ministry, we pray.

Amen.

~~~~~~~
~~~~~~~

Lord's Supper

Who is this on the cross,
Hanging like a nobody?
Looking on humanity,
With so much love?
Feeling their agony,
As none could?

He is Christ Jesus,
The Son of God,
Love personified,
Compassion embodied.

Come to us again,
Risen Savior,
Dine with us around the table,
Remind us of your blood and shame,
That brought us life eternal.

In your visitation,
Take away our sins and guilt,
Pardon our arrogance,
And bring us to Paradise. Amen.

Holy Lord,
We come to your table,
A symbol of redemption,
So precious;
For it cost you your life.

We come to your table,
A sign of communion,
So rare;
For only in you there is unity.

We come to your table,
An example of supreme sacrifice,
So perfect;
For only you can show us such love.

Thanks be you, lord Jesus. Amen.

Gracious God,
Thank you for thinking about us,
When we have forgotten our sinfulness before your holiness.

Thank you for sending your beloved Son,
A spotless lamb for our blemished souls.

Thank you for accepting his self-sacrifice,
An estranged people thus forgiven and reconciled with you.

For Children in the Womb

ONE: Loving God,

ALL: Grant us wisdom that we may discern your will for all the babies in the womb that we may choose that which is according to your perfect will and not in accordance with our selfish quest for comfort and conformity to social and cultural tastes.

ONE: Loving God,

ALL: Grant us grace to embrace every life with joy, knowing fully well that the child in the womb is a seed waiting to become a tree that will bear fruit to multiply and fill the earth.

ONE: Loving God,

ALL: Grant us vision to behold the face and future of every unborn child, seeing that one could be an ancestor of a thousand like an Abraham and a Sarah, or like a Shiphrah, a Puah and a Moses become champions of liberating those in bondage. And that they could be like a Deborah or a Solomon who epitomizes wisdom in times of fear and doubt. And also that they could be any of the Marys who birth a Savior, who served Jesus at his feet, and witnessed to the Gospel of Jesus' resurrection.

ONE: We ask these in Jesus' name

ALL: Amen.

For Parenthood

God our parent,
Show us to be like you,
The mother who gives birth,
Nurtures, dandles, holds us to your breast, and constantly gathers your children.

Teach us to be like you,
The father who protects,
Defends, corrects, and guides us with love in the way of truth and justice.

In our speaking,
Give us wisdom,
In our conduct,
Give us grace.
In everything,
Help us mirror your parenthood.
Amen.

Father's Day Prayer

Our father in heaven,
Our source of strength, confidence and security.

Thank you for earthly fathers,
Who reflect your character,
And stand as fortresses for the family.

Grant solace to them when strained by family problems,
Discernment when perplexed by life's circumstances,
And joy in discovering beauty in every work of your hands.

By your wise counsel,
Lead our fathers on earth
To be teachers of truth,
Models of righteousness,
And living legacies of purity,
In their family, the church and community.

For those among us who are without fathers,
Send fatherly figures along their way,
That their longings for a father may be satisfied in ways you best provide.

As children of our fathers,
Give us hearts that are grateful,
To recount the sacrifice of selflessness they've made for our better future.
In Christ, your perfect son's name, we pray.
Amen.

Mother's Day Prayer

God, who is like our mother,
You give us life,
Nurtures, feeds and ties the family.

Thank you for earthly mothers,
Who are like you in many ways –
Co-procreators and sustainers of precious lives.

Thank you for them, who sacrifice their comforts and dreams, even their bodies,
To multiply and fill the earth, as you have commanded.

May the fruit/s of her womb rise to honor her,
And may she rejoice in them.

Clothe her with strength and confidence in a way that only you can,
And so adorned, may she walk the road of motherhood with dignity and steadfast faith.

To those children without mothers,
Come to them O mothering God,
And fill all void created by their absence.

Grant good health and long life to all mothers in our midst,
And your abiding peace and joy go with them today and onto eternity.

With thanksgiving in Jesus' name we pray. Amen.

****

ONE: God of Moses, you discriminate not one of your children but calls them by name to be your witness.

ALL: Praise be to you O righteous God.

ONE: You chose Moses to be a deliverer and when he needed an eloquent tongue you despised him not but sent Aaron to serve as his mouthpiece to fulfill your mission.

ALL: Praise be to you O faithful God.

ONE: Christ Jesus, you leave none out in your healing ministry. You make the crippled walk, the blind see, paralytic stand, the mute speak, restore withered hands and make the maimed whole.

ALL: Praise be to you O compassionate Lord

ONE: Even when you were reviled and ridiculed, you approved their faith and silenced the cruel judgments against them.

ALL: Praise be to you O loving Lord.

ONE: Holy Spirit, with you in them, the apostles and all faithfuls receive power to continue the restorative work of Jesus Christ.

ALL: Praise be to you O power divine.

ONE: Even in the reality of the inevitable thorn in the flesh of Paul, you perfectly manifested your power through him and accomplish great works till this day.

ALL: Praise to you O God the Spirit.

ONE: Jesus Christ, Lord of the Church, you make the entire humanity one body in you, our head. All of us as members in your once broken body on the Cross receive wholeness. Change any thought in us that regards a member to be inferior or dispensable so that no individual member may suffer discrimination. Thus let your body remain unbroken till our unity is perfected in eternity.

ALL: Amen.

(Cf., Ex 3-4; Lk; Matt 9: 2-7, 32-33; 12: 9-13; 2Cor 12: 7b-9; 1Cor 12)

::::::::::::::

Disabled Manifesto

Lord, my maker, let your Spirit descend upon me,
And anoint me to bring good news to those in poverty of any kind.
Send me to proclaim release to those captivated by prejudices and disabled-phobia,
Recovery of sight to those blinded by pride and hypocrisy,
To let the socially, politically, economically and religiously oppressed go free,
And to proclaim the Jubilee message of kindness, dignity and liberty.

Neither take away your Spirit nor your gifts and calling from me.
Make my disability reflect your impartiality,
And make me a living model of your compassion and justice.
In the name of Jesus our redeemer.
Amen.

(Inspired by Lk 4: 18-19)

::::::::::::::

CELEBRATIONS

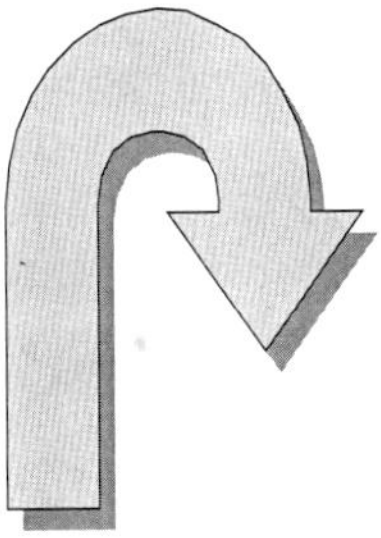

I

New Beginnings

God of all ages, as the New Year begins,
Open our eyes to see the yearlong road ahead,
That we may not miss to see the signposts that you have placed on our way.

Help us to be a Good Samaritan,
Willing to descend from our ride of comfort,
And to lend our helping hands to those who are wounded – heart and soul,
And in you to give of our time and resources to restore them back to life.

Help us to be a Peter and a John,
That even when we have nothing, except the gifts from you,

We would be willing to put the weak and downtrodden on their feet with the words,
"Silver and gold have I none, but what I have I give you;
In the name of Jesus Christ of Nazareth, stand up and walk."

Help us to be a Dorcas,
That we would be generous for your name's sake,
And through us poor widows, orphans and destitute,
Find reason to believe in your love;
Raise us up like her to do gracious work.

Help us to be like Jesus,
Who continues to care, heal, and suffer -
With the sorrowing, the diseased, and the marginalized.
Let your Holy Spirit descend upon us,
To enable us to do the things he did.

And may all glory be yours. Amen

(Cf., Jn 4: 1-42; Acts 3:1-10; 9: 36-42; Lk 4: 18-19)

II

Fresh Resolve

ONE: God, who makes all things new,
ALL: Grant mercy for all that calls for your forgiveness –

ONE: For sins unacknowledged,
For good deeds left undone;
ALL: Grant mercy for all that calls for your forgiveness.

ONE: For thoughtless words that offend,
For kind speech unspoken;
ALL: Grant mercy for all that calls for your forgiveness.
ONE: For motives that destroy,
For truth not practiced in love;
ALL: Grant mercy for all that calls for your forgiveness.

ONE: For selfish pursuits and greedy acts,
For hands and feet unused in the service of others;
ALL: Grant mercy for all that calls for your forgiveness.

ONE: Forgiven in Jesus' name, cause us to travel the year with you Almighty God;
ALL: And in doing so, may our year be a year that satisfies your desire for us. Amen.

III
Renewal

Spirit of God,
Visit your people today as you did Jesus on the day of his Baptism,
And thus reaffirm your delight in us in these your words: "These are my beloved children with whom I am well pleased!"

Renew us inside out that we may be born anew in body and Spirit,
And thus help us enter your domain of steadfast love, faithfulness, righteousness and peace.

Restore our hope for now and to eternity,
And thus make our lives meaningful for ourselves and all else.

In Jesus Christ, who is the same yesterday and today and forever the same, we pray. Amen.

(Cf. Matt 3: 16-17; Jn 3: 3-7; Ps 85: 10-11; Heb 13: 8)

******

I

God of Eve and Adam,
Two lives you make one,
Two hearts you link together,
Two souls you join in unison,
To love, to hold and to cherish forever.
Thanks be to you in Jesus' name.
Amen.

II

God of Love,
May these two lives find –
Your hand upon their hands,
Your Spirit upon their spirits,

May they find –
Strength in your joy,
Peace in your presence,
Fullness in your righteousness.
Amen.

III

Merciful God,
Grant that your two children from today -
Will be patient when angry,
Kind when upset,
Loving when envious,
Humble when arrogant,
Understanding when irritable,
Trusting when doubtful,
And hopeful when down.

And in being so –
Let the strength in the one perfect the
weakness in the other.
To the honor of your name.
Amen.

IV

May the two you have joined together,
Rejoice in each other,
Believe in the other,
Hope in each other's best,

Endure all trials,
Bear each other's burdens,
Making their marriage last.
Amen.

V

The Lord bless this man and this woman,
To esteem the other better than the self,
To listen to the other with humility,
To speak with respect,
To be tolerant of each other's opinion,
To not insist on one's own way,
To allow each to flourish,
And from them may the fruits of godly marriage
nourish those whose are stressed for growth.
Amen.

VI

On this holy matrimonial occasion, we pray for
grace on your daughter and son to -
Look with love,
Serve with gratitude,

Live in harmony,
Grow in strength;

May words be honest but gentle,
Intentions be straight but pure,
Attitudes be clear but honorable,
Actions be assertive but respectful.

Knowing fully well that in thinking well of the other, they think good for themselves.
In Christ we pray. Amen.

VII

God of the ages,
What you have joined,
Let no one and nothing separate,
May their eyes behold beauty only in each other;
May their hearts have room only for the other;
May their marriage bed remain pure.

May they not grow weary of each other,
But fall in love a thousand times over;
Waiting more on each other with every passing day.

May you, the unchanging God make this possible
for them from this moment on.
Through the Holy Spirit, we pray. Amen.

VIII

Lord God,
On this day _________ (wedding date)
We pray for your blessings on these two souls;
That their union may be pleasant as precious oil
running down upon the beard of Aaron.
And nourishing like the dew of Hermon which
falls on the mountains of Zion.
Today may you ordain blessing and joy evermore.
Amen.

(Adapted from Ps 133)

IX

Minister: God of Creation,
Bride&Groom: We thank you for bringing us
together.
Minister: As the two join in holy marriage and
begin their life as one,
Bride&Groom: Grant us all we need to make our
lives together as good as you intend for us.

Minister: In every circumstance,
Bride& Groom: Tighten our bond that we may keep each other up, close and strong.
Minister: Even towards the end of life's journey,
Bride&Groom: May we still find ourselves beside each other.
ALL: Amen.

X

Gracious God,
Look with favor on these that were two but now have become as one,
That love for another increase and for self may decrease;
That prosperity be multiplied and poverty removed;
That offspring visit and sufferings vanish;
That friendship abound and resentment distant;
That kith and kin celebrate and none dejected.
In Jesus' name, Amen.

XI

God our provider,
You have given us this day to rejoice with this man and woman;
We now ask that you will give them many reasons to delight in their life ahead.
Give grace if they falter,
Hope if they suffer,
Resources if they need,
Joy if they sadden,
Success if they labor,
Peace if they yearn,
Health if they pray,
Length of days if they ask,
Offspring if it's in your will.
Amen.

XII

All knowing God,
May what you have joined together be never put asunder;
By anything and anyone,
In any season and time.
Amen.

XIII

(Prayer by bride and groom)
God of Love,
May my heart stay true to this one person
You've handpicked for me.
May the journey ahead with him/her,
Be in step with you and with each other.
May the joys and sorrows of life,
Take us up and down together but never apart.
For Christ's sake, Amen.

XIV

God of all beginnings,
Even as the groom and bride has sought to be united,
May you help them seek to be united with you before all else.
In Christ we ask.
Amen

******

1.

God be in every pillar and beams of the house,
God's blessing flow in from the windows,
And go out with joy through every door.

All those who pass by this dwelling,
See beauty not only in its walls and floors,
But also the charm that emanates from inside.

All who visit this house see God residing in it,
Because it has opened its heart of generosity,
And extended its hand of hospitality.

Through rain or sunshine,
And through life's toughest days,
May this house stand to bear you witness.
Amen.

2.

May God hold the foundation of this place in his strong hands,
May his watchful eyes be upon this house at all times,
May his glorious face be turned towards it every-day.

May those who live herein –
Be sheltered from storm and thunder,
Protected from mishaps and losses,
Passed by, by sorrow and evil.

May each day bring peace as the day before,
Health and prosperity be a constant companion,
Mornings be as blissful as the nights,
And the nights as the days.

May the flowers, trees and vegetation around it flourish,
That all may eat of the fruits of your plentiful provisions,
And be nourished to a life of humility and grati-tude.
Amen.

3.

God of our Ancestor Solomon,
We beseech your favor for this house as did Solomon when he built the Temple for all nations.

We pray, like him, that your eyes will be open night and day toward this house,
That this house will initiate reconciliation,
And forgiveness will walk out from here.

That prayers and praises will abound at all times and seasons,
And friends and strangers meet to celebrate your name,
And say, "God is truly in this home!"

In Jesus' name, Amen.

(Inspired by 1Kgs 8: 22-52)

The name shall be___

God of creation,
Breathe life in abundance on this your child,
That s/he may live up to his/her name,
Speaking life to every dry bone,
Invoking breath into them,
And bringing them up from the graves;
To the honor of your name. Amen.

(Cf., Ezek 37)

^^^^^^^

Minister: We lift up this child to you,
That like Jesus s/he would grow in wisdom and in stature, favored by you and neighbors.
Parents: Help us God.

Minister: We place him/her to your care,
That s/he would have no gods apart from you but worship you only, loving you keeping your commandments.
Parents: Help us God.

Minister: We dedicate her/his life into your service, That where and when you call s/he would respond promptly and follow your lead.
Parents: Help us God.

Minister: We trust your faithfulness to rest upon him/her,
That all along life's journey you will constantly abide with him/her, giving counsel and keeping temptations at bay.
Parents: Help us God.

Minister: The Triune God go with you from this day forth till eternity.
All: Amen.

(Lk 2: 52; Ex 20: 2-6)

^^^^^^^

Spirit of Life,
This child is your own;
S/he is alive because you provide the breath of life.

Savior of Life,
This child has become yours;
S/he lives free because you redeemed her/him from sin and death.

Source of Life,
This child is your handiwork;
S/he owes life to you and derives purpose from you only.

Triune God,
Grant abundance of life and reward of fruitfulness;
S/he has only so long to live witnessing your grace.
Amen.

^^^^^^

Thank you God of all lives,
For the joy of life channeled through _________
(name of birthday person).

Allow him/her to grow in you with each passing year.

In Christ alone we pray. Amen.

//////////\\\\\\\\\\

God of life,
Birthdays come and they go,
We continue to live the days in between;
Praying that you will make each day as celebratory as the day of birth.
With gratitude in the name of Jesus Christ, we pray. Amen.

//////////\\\\\\\\\\

My life is a gift from your, God my Creator,
I'm wonderfully made in your image,
Although sinful you have redeemed me in your Son Jesus.

So grant me life in abundance,
And complete your work of salvation in me,
That I may live my life everyday remembering your goodness with thanksgiving.
Amen.

//////////\\\\\\\\\\

May God Almighty,
Breathe his Spirit on you again this day, as he did on the day you were conceived in your mother's womb.

May Christ the Savior,
Give you a long and meaningful life.
May the Holy Spirit,
Keep you from falling into the pit of lifelessness.

In every step of your way,
May the triune God –
Be the spring of your joy,
Your hope,
And your goal.
Amen.

//////////\\\\\\\\\\

Wedding - a

On this 25th[1] anniversary of our union,
We recall your goodness upon us, dear Lord.
You've upheld our faith in sorrow as in joy,
You've brought us nearer in sickness as in health,
You've strengthened our bond in calamity as in success,
You've walked with us through life's mountains as through its valleys,
Let all glory and thanks be to you.
Amen.

Wedding – b

O Lord God, what more can we ask?
Your providence has met our heart's desires and more.
You lengthened our span of life together,
And stretched it longer with precious offspring.

[1] Change the number according to personal occasion.

You relate with us,
And extend that relationship with family ties.

You give us your grace,
And bountifully pour out its goodness in our daily living.

You provided for us in the past,
And continues to be our hope for the future.

May your name be praised forever! Amen.

Wedding – c

What can we give you when you are Lord over all?
But in meekness accept our gratitude for –
Enriching our lives together as wife and husband,
Children and grandchildren[2] to fill up any empty space between us,
Peace when prayers were responded in your way not ours,
Joy when as a couple we accomplished feats unimaginable for one of us to have done alone,
Moments like this to look back on our journey so far and also to look forward to the road ahead....

---

[2] Can add or omit as may be relevant.

May you be glorified in our lives, for Christ's sake. Amen.

Wedding – d

Walk with us Lord,
Speak words of wisdom,
Breathe life into our relationship,
And as you have in the past, so in the coming days allow us to celebrate this occasion.
In Jesus' name we pray. Amen.

Wedding - e

God, forever three in One,
Let your steadfast love be our food,
Your merciful grace be our drink,
And your abiding presence the air.
Then we shall continue to grow in you and in each other. Amen.

Institution – a

O God, this institution[3] bears your stamp of approval.
You have sustained it for the past _____ (relevant number) years.

Today we can only thank you –
For allowing the difficult times that were outnumbered by blessed days;
For despair that were met by your unfailing providence;
For mistakes that were overwritten by your faithful mercy;
For enemies that were turned to reliable partners;
For well wishers that have remained valuable assets.

May your name be praised through this institution in Christ Jesus.
Amen.

[3] The name of the school, office, social service centre, program, magazine etc., can be inserted.

Institution – b

ONE: God, our firm foundation,

To you we credit the establishment of this ______ (name of institution).

We remember with gladness the pioneers of this institution who exemplified great faith in its value:

In every brick that was laid with hope,
In every step taken to where it is today,
In every cent/paise that was donated to build it,
In every person who prayed for its success.

ALL: We ask your peace upon them.

ONE: There are those who planted the seed but have gone before us to be in their eternal home, before its fruition, we invoke your kindness on their household.

Let them reap rich harvest from your field of plenty, for the sake of their ancestors who labored hard for this place.

ALL: We ask your peace upon them.

ONE: Those who are in leadership now and those who will come later, we pronounce blessings of wisdom, endurance and selflessness.

Every decision made, and action taken and planned, be an evidence of an answer to the benediction for the sake of Jesus Christ. Amen.

Church –a

To the God who built this Church upon the foundation of Christ, our Redeemer,
Be glory forever in this Church and in the Church universal.

To Jesus, the eternal Christ, who loved his 'body' and gave his life for it,
Be thanks forever in this Church and in the Church universal.

To the Holy Spirit, who nourishes the body and prepares her as a holy bride of Christ,
Be power forever in this Church and in the Church universal. Amen.

Church –b

O God, has this church done enough to bring you honor?

Has it established your reign far enough?

Has it labored enough to find the least and the lost among your children?

Has it loved its members enough to mirror the love of Christ?

Help us this day to renew our calling to fulfill the purpose of being a Church.

In unity of faith, make us a people that obey its head, our Savior and Jesus Christ.

Wherever she is, cause your justice and mercy to become reality.

Keep her ever free from sin and evil; made ready to return to your holy presence. Amen.

I

God of wisdom,
You are the spring from which all knowledge flows.

You provide understanding,
And bestow ability to undertake written tests and oral interviews.
And most of all you alone give success.

We thank you for the opportunity to begin new task as a ________________ (office/designation/responsibility).

As you have opened the door,
So also guide us through the corridors of our work,
That we may not stumble against the trappings of the evil one;
But with your light of wisdom ever going before and never behind,
Lead me[1] through to excellence,
For your name's sake.
Amen.

---

[1] Can be prayed by an individual, in a group or the minister can say it on behalf of the successful candidate; the personal pronouns can be changed accordingly.

II

God Almighty,
We acknowledge that –

The sun does not shine by its might,
Nor the moon by its will.

The river neither flows by its pleasurable course,
Nor the trees blossom by its own strength.

The student labors not,
Nor reaps the fruit of success by capable force.

You are the Cause of all,
And you make our plans to prosper.

You generated the will to pursue,
And the power to believe in accomplishment.

You provided energy to learn,
And understanding to reproduce knowledge.

May all glory be yours,
Today and in the days ahead.
Amen.

III

Thank you for the light,
That enables us to see and study;

Thank you for the mind,
That helps us understand our lessons;

Thank you for the food,
That keeps us strong to sit and read;

Thank you for the commutes to and fro,
That takes us to schools and back;

Thank you for those who watch over us,
They ensure our waking and sleeping times;

Thank you for the teacher,
They teach and labor till we get it;

Thank you for the knowledge,
It keeps us grounded on you, O Sophia.
Amen.

SOLEMN MOMENTS

God of Life,
You give and take,
You are absolute.
Though it's hard to let go of our loved ones,
Keep us rejoicing that they return to you for eternity.
In Jesus, the prince of peace, we pray. Amen.

God, our counselor,
Comfort us with the peace beyond worldly ability,
Just like the one with which you comforted the disciples of Jesus when he was to leave them for an eternal purpose.
We need you greatly than at all other times,
So be gracious and leave us not.
Amen.

(Cf., Jn 14)

Minister
From the beginning of time, you are Lord.
In life as in death you are Lord.
You change not and your plans for us remain in suffering and in joy.
We commit the spirit of your beloved child______ (name of the deceased).

Receive her/him into your arms and glorify him/ her according to the riches of your compassion.

Honor the family with your benevolence that even when their hearts are breaking, enable them to be content in knowing that his/her journey on earth had been fruitful. Also, help the family to cherish the good legacies that______ (name of deceased) has left for them to emulate.

And to all who must continue our earthy journey, remind us to love you and one another that we may ultimately live with you and with our loved ones for all eternity.

In the blessed name of Christ Jesus, we pray. Amen.

Minister

Blessed are you, O Lord our Maker,
At the dawn of life when we are born, you are there because we could not be alive unless you willed it.
At the afternoon of life when youthfulness adorns, you are there because we could not succeed in life unless you favored us.
At the sunset of life when age catches up on us, you are there because we could not get there unless you blessed our days.

In all stages of life, you are there; being Lord of all lives.

The family of ______ (name of deceased) mourns the end of his/her day on earth. Let the day spent in your presence by him/her be a constant reminder to the family of the beauty of life with you. As you have been with him/her throughout the day, so continue to let him/her sleep in the most peaceful manner perceivable to human, until s/he awakes at your coming to be reunited with you, family, friends and all who have gone before him/her.

In the name of Christ, our redeemer, we pray. Amen.

God, in our sorrowing moments, you are our peace and hope.
The silence of ________ (name of deceased) is so loud it breaks our hearts.
The vacuum s/he leaves is so wide no one would fit in.
The sweet memory s/he leaves behind is so bitter nothing would sweeten.
Mend our brokenness, fill our emptiness, and satisfy our longings.
And may s/he rest in your bosom until we meet again because of your Son, our Saviour Jesus.
Amen.

Our faithful Shepherd,
We walk today through the valley of death.

Sadness overwhelms us,
Fear grips us,
Loneliness envelops us.

Tears are overflowing,
Hearts are breaking,
Spirits are dying inside.

Yet, we hope in you even in the darkest valley,
Your rod and staff of grace will comfort us,
Your presence will ease the agony.

Amen.

(Cf., Ps 23)

Almighty God,
You come to us in your power,
Through the forces of nature.

And we humbly acknowledge your Lordship over all,
As much as we ask your pardon if our neglect of earth has brought this fury upon us.

But today we mourn with and for those who are affected by ______________ (name calamity such as flood, landslide, earthquake, fire etc.),
They are innocent and need your mercy to rebuild their lives.

Restore their broken homes and properties in ways that only you can help for we cannot even begin to think of its possibility.

In your wisdom and loving ways,
Enable them to look beyond the tragedy,
Towards the joy of new beginnings.
In Jesus' name we pray, Amen.

>>>>><<<<<

God of the land, the sea, the sky,
You have the whole universe in your hand for it is duly yours.
You sent your begotten Son to save the world and all that is in it,
And yet at this moment, destruction has surrounded us,
We know not what to make of it;
Is it your will for us to suffer or to repent?
Or is it your way of showing your love in the midst of the inevitable?
Let not our confusion lead to unbelief,
Help us to trust you even more...
For Christ's sake, Amen.

>>>>><<<<<

Hospitalization

Christ, the Great healer,
You are the ultimate physician,
You touch and diseases disappear,
You speak and demons leave,
You will and people are made whole.

Please will your healing on _____ (name of patient),
And let your restorative work in her/him be a living testimony of your grace.
Amen.

****

God from whom life flows,
Pour out your gift of health on your child _____ (name of patient).

Use the doctors and nurses as channels of your merciful healing.

Grant care givers the joy of rendering service to her/him as if unto you.

Send empathizing companions to encourage him/her even without saying a word.

Meet all their financial needs for right treatment, and grateful hearts to accept generosity of kith and kin, friends and strangers.

Let the counselor, the Holy Spirit, be ever near her/him to grant hope and increase in faith; through Christ the eternal One we pray. Amen.

****

In sickness as in health,
In want as in plenty,
In bed as in motion,
In hospital as at home,
Lord, grant me grace to hope in your timely touch on my body. Amen.

****

Holy Spirit, our source of comfort,
As I lay sick in bed,
Attend to me,
Abide with me.
Come to me in the doctor,
The nurse,
The visitor.

Remove doubts and fears,
From my mind,
My spirit,
My heart.

Restore to me the joy of your peace,
Let it remain,
Till it becomes mine forever.
Amen.

MINISTRY INDUCTION

ONE

The one who called you to pastoral work is the true Shepherd of the Sheep,

PASTOR

Help me God to depend on you alone.

ONE

The one who died for the flock you will now tend is his bride,

PASTOR

Help me Jesus to prepare her for the consummation of the union with you in glory.

ONE

The one who nurtures all under your care is the teacher of truth,

PASTOR

Help me Spirit to yield to your counsel.

ONE

The triune God will guide you, protect and embolden you as long as you keep our eyes on the sheep and lead them safely home.

PASTOR

God help me.

ALL

Amen.

☆

Shepherd's Confidence

Your flock is in my care;
I am but only a guardian.
You are the true Shepherd;
I will follow the Staff of your Spirit to lead me.

I fear the wolves of earthly pleasures seeking to devour your lambs;
I doubt my prowess to protect them.
You are the true Shepherd;
Raise your Staff and part them asunder.

I fear the thieves of modern cults seeking to steal them away from you;
I doubt my wisdom to keep them.
You are the true Shepherd;
Raise your Staff and squash their plans.
I fear the danger of complacence in performing routine tasks;
I doubt my passion to sustain me.
You are the true Shepherd;
Raise your Staff and walk with me everyday.

☆

Shepherd's Vow

PASTOR

I take you flock of God under my care from this day forth:
To feed you with truth,
To guide you with wisdom,
To love you with purity,
To rebuke you with love,
To discipline you with gentleness.
To mourn with you when sad,

To be companion when afraid,
To lift you when down,
To direct you when lost,
To counsel you when perplexed.
To ever be trustworthy,
Daily be diligent,
Always available,
Constantly discerning,
Ever visionary.
Not causing one little one to be lost,
To fall into the devil's snare,
To slip and stumble along the way,
To feel abandoned,
To look for another home.
Not of my own power,
Not of my own strength,
Neither of my wealth,
Nor of my talent,
Only of Christ – the Good Shepherd.

ALL

So God help you.
Amen

☆

Shepherd's Prayer

Holy God,

In Jesus Christ,

Let my aspiration to the task of a Pastor live up to his image as the perfect high priest.

Help me live above reproach,

Practicing fidelity in marriage,

Not consumed by anger,

Sensible in every situation,

Earning the respect of the people,

Willing to open my heart and home,

Dutiful in teaching,

Sober at all times,

Building peace,

Not a lover of money,

Training my children in the way of the Lord.

Amen.

☆

Blessings on Pastors

I

God grant you –

Compassion to understand the hurt in even the least of your sheep,

Wisdom to attend to the one that went astray, not forgetting the ones on-course,

Humility to regard everyone as equal,

Generosity to offer oneself to the service of the Almighty God – in this church and beyond,

Now and to eternity. Amen.

II

The Spirit of God indwell you from above,

Move you from within to without,

Charge you to selflessness,

In the kenotic power of Christ, the lamb of God,

To the glory of God. Amen.

III

May your heart be restless till all the members of the church find rest in God,

May your mind be empty of self till every nation understands Jesus as everything,

May your strength be weakened till the whole world knows the pervasive presence of the Spirit .

Amen.

IV

Be a pastor that tends to the sheep, not the wolves;

Be a servant that obeys the master, not money;

Be a minster that serves the people, not the powerful;

In everything seek the glory of God, not of self.

And he will keep you from falling till he returns to give you a share in his glory.

Amen.

V

The Lord grant you –

Courage when afraid,

Peace when anxious,

And a friend when troubled,

When nothing makes a difference,

may he be Immanuel – God with you –

to the awesome praise of his grace.

Amen.

VI

May you be a light for the whole of creation,

That those who walk in darkness may find their way back to the path of salvation,

In the power of the Spirit, to the glory of God and honor of Christ Jesus.

Amen.

*****

In Service

MINISTER

God, you have appointed these people to serve the Church. Let them now mirror the serving nature of our Lord Jesus Christ, to whose name they bear witness. Let them be full of the Holy Spirit because only by his presence in them, they will accomplish the task of deaconship.

DEACONS

Help us to serve in reverence of the Trinity.

MINISTER

Grant them faith that moves them to action. Let them to be quick to hear the pleas of the needy. Let them humbly hasten to assist those that devote themselves to serving the Word and Sacraments.

DEACONS

Help us to serve in the power of the Trinity.

MINISTER

Strengthen them to a life of integrity. Let them serve you and the people well. Let them gain good standing for themselves. Let them gain favor in your sight as well.

DEACONS

Help us to serve in a manner worthy of the holy Trinity. Amen.

DEACONS' PRAYER

Lord of the Church,
In the enabling power of the Holy Spirit –
Keep us diligent and honest,
Not indulging in alcohol,
Not greedy for wealth,
Pleasant at all times,
Faithful to our spouse,
Attentive to our children,
Excelling in managing household,
A firm believer in the Gospel.

In the grace of Jesus Christ –
Put us to the test,
Prove us blameless,
Accept us in your service as deacons. Amen.

(Inspired by 1Tim 3: 8-12)

USHER'S PRAYER

God, our Creator,
As I discharge my responsibility as an [1]usher/steward,
Let my sight be not only on the rich and glamorous,
Let not my heart covet the offerings that are yours,
Let not my presence be to gain attention.

Help me be courteous to those with branded suits as well as *khadi* shirts,
Help me lend a hand to those in stilettos as well as rubber shoes,
Help me be kind to those who bring heavy gifts as well as those who can only offer a [2]widow's mite.

Make me a friend to both strangers and acquaintances,
A joyful steward of your resources,
A humble servant to your church and the world. Amen.

◇

---

[1] Whichever word or any word that may be relevant to the church/context. This prayer is especially directed to ushers in a worship context.
[2] Lk 20: 1-4.

Minster

God over all, we dedicate these - your children to serve you as stewards and ushers.

Stewards/Ushers

We joyfully commit ourselves to you.

Minister

Grant integrity, diligence and wisdom to execute their responsibilities well.

Stewards/Ushers

We fully commit ourselves to you.

Minister

Use their hands, feet, heart and mind to reflect the servanthood attitude of our Savior Jesus Christ.

Stewards/Ushers

We humbly commit ourselves to you.

Minister

Let your Holy Spirit abide within them and make them fruitful in church, at home and in workplace.

Stewards/Ushers

We confidently commit ourselves to you.

All

Let the community be blessed by their service. Amen.

Choir

ONE: God of all good things, we give you glory for the gift of music and for those who speak your words through it,

CHOIR: Accept our voices as an offering.

ONE: We give you thanks for the musicians and conductor, who inspires and guides the singers,

CHOIR: Accept our talents as an offering.

ONE: We honor you for the hours of rehearsals that the team will put in to make you known,

CHOIR: Accept our commitment to praise you.

ONE: We dedicate all members for your holy purpose,

CHOIR: Accept our all and make it wholly yours to use.

ONE: To all eternity may the best music be lifted up to you on earth and in heaven.

ALL: Amen.

ONE: The breeze whispers,
The wind gushes,
The storm surges,
The lightning sparkles,

Each sounding as though -
a gentle alto,
a fierce bass,
a passionate soprano,
an ardent tenor.

Together sounding as though –
In perfect harmony,
Not one claiming prominence,
Not one faltering to do its part,
Each fulfilling its purpose.

As rain falls after its full course,
To quench the earth below,
And to make it fruitful;
So may your songs be:
To cause God's people to grow.

CHOIR: May we ever seek the same. Amen.

^^^^^^^^^^^^^^^^^^^^^^

MINISTER:

The voices that we dedicate this day,

be to you,

your people's grateful offering;

and to your people,

your gracious gift of a fountain of joy.

CHOIR:

Bless us to bless you and your people. Amen

^^^^^^^^^^^^^^^^^^^^^^^^

MINISTER

Let the Spirit breathe within you the peace of Jesus that your voices will find a home in the hearts of the people, causing them to turn to their author and perfecter of faith, our Savior Jesus Christ.

CHOIR

Breathe on us Holy Spirit, to the glory of God. Amen.

^^^^^^^^^^^^^^^^^^^^^

CHOIR

May our lives be to you an offering as genuine as the music we sing,

And our minds blend with yours as the harmony of the tiny flute with the giant harp,

In simplicity and exquisiteness of our melody, let our desire be only to glorify you.

Amen.

^^^^^^^^^^^^^^^^^^^

Minister

God who created everyone in your image, we acknowledge the commitment of your servants to instruct the children in your ways.

Instructors

Thank your for the calling.

Minister

Christ who love everyone the same, we surrender these disciples of yours to help them show love to all children under their spiritual care.

Instructors

Thank you for your examples.

Minster

Spirit who is the teacher of truth, we entrust these earthly teachers to your wisdom believing that you will guide them to impart truthful knowledge to the little ones.

Instructors

Thank you for your counsel.

Minister

May God's kingdom descend upon this church and everywhere through the ministry to children.

All

To the glory and honor of the Triune God. Amen.

Sunday School Teacher's Praise

Almighty God,
How tender are your deeds!
You forgive without reserve,
And like children who easily abandon a grudge, you promise to remember our sins no more!

How lovely it is to be your child!
You love without bias,
And like children who mingle without prejudice, you embrace all peoples as your own!

How privileged it is to be in your service!
You call despite our emptiness,
And like children eager to be filled with knowledge, you supply our needs to the full!

Blessed be to your name! Amen

FAREWELLS

R

Blessed be the God of life,
Who endows health to complete professional tasks,
Provides satisfaction in doing assigned jobs,
Sends colleagues to work as teammates,
Blesses with friends to walk tough spots together,
Grants years to finish a journey....
Amen.

God of yesterday,
How needlessly I wondered:
"What did the future hold for me!?"
Now I stand as a testament to your leading.

God of today,
How anxiously I keep asking:
"What does the present have for me?"
Now I stand waiting for you to lead me on.

God of tomorrow,
How fearfully I question:
"What will the future bring me?"
Now I stand to ask remembrance of your leading.

In the name of Jesus who is the same forever,
I pray, Amen.

Lord,
Help me see your hand on my past,
Your heart on my todays and,
Your eyes on my tomorrows.

Let what I have seen of you before,
Be a lamp of trust to me now,
And a light of hope forever. Amen.

God,
Thank you that you gave me a life long enough to see this retirement day,

Thank you that you were there when I was fruitful,
And even when I seemed fruitless.

Thank you that you will continue to grow with me,
Pruning me along the way that I may bear some more fruit.

Thank you that this day is not the end of my life,
But a beginning for 'bound'less opportunities in your service.

Thank you that your grace on me enables me to hope and fulfill your plans.
Amen.

Lord of all nations and places on earth,
You know our steps even before we take the first one,
We believe you brought us to ____ (place of leaving),
And now we trust you to lead us to _____ (place of moving).
Any unforeseen lack in preparation that may hinder us from a smooth transition, we pray your grace to provide.
For we ask in the name of your Son who left heaven for earth. Amen.

God, who fills the earth,
By your gracious providence,
Provide us decent home for the family to share our lives,
Kind neighborhood to mutually flourish,
New friends to enrich our days,
Credible school for the children for virtuous growth,
And a church to worship you and mature into your likeness.
Through Jesus in the Holy Spirit we pray.
Amen.

God,
Lead us out of the fear of the unknown,
Into your realm of omniscience,
That we may hope in your goodness to provide our needs demanded by a new location.

Even when doubt creeps inside,
Remind us of your faithfulness,
That we may obediently submit to your plans that always mysteriously works for our good.
To you be glory in this place and everywhere.
Amen.

New workplace, school and neighborhood,
Changed climate, culture and relationships,
Fresh assignments, experiences and challenges,
Lord, we bring them into your merciful hand;
Take them and turn them, for us, into opportunities for a fuller life.
Amen.

God who guided Abraham and Sarah to Haran from the land of Ur,
And from Haran to Canaan,
So journey with us,

Deliver us from evil ways,
Prosper us for your name's sake.

Grant us success in the land you are taking us,
Make us channels of your Sun of righteousness,
That any sign of descending darkness,
May be overpowered by the brightness of your Light,
Help us carry your light in the corner we will live.

Amen.

(Cf., Gen 11-15)

God, What are we but sojourners,
Travelling this side of the world to another,
In body as it is in Spirit.

We remain where you put us,
And move when you bid us go,
In the past as it is in the now.

Yet you have been constant,
You have never failed to stand by us,
In sorrow as it is in happiness.

We yield ourselves to your pleasure,
Knowing fully well your perfect plan for us,
In distant land as it is in this place.

Keep us close to your will,
That we may not stop short of attaining your blessings,
In weakness as it is in strength.

To the glory and honor of Christ,
Our Friend, Savior and Lord. Amen.

Holy Spirit Divine,
You blow where you choose,
We know not where you come from or where you go,
But we know you are there,
In every heart and every place establishing the reign of God.

Abide with us too,
That in you we may partake and be part of the mission of building God's domain in every corner of the world.
Amen.

(Cf., Jn 3: 1-8)

God of the earth, sky and sea,
Take control of all things around as we travel from _____ (place of boarding) to _____ (place of arrival).
As you calmed the raging sea of Galilee, so calm our minds to trust that all of nature obeys your command, through Christ our peace we pray. Amen.

(Cf., Mk 4:35-41)

+++++++

God, by your providence, watch over our baggage, as much as you do over our transport and our lives. Amen.

+++++++

God from ancient days,
Let your angels meet us on every bend;

Grant us wisdom to stay on the safe lane and be awake to heights and slopes;

Send your Spirit to be a pillar of fire by night and on foggy stretches, and a pillar of cloud in scorching heat;

...Till our destination is arrived upon.
In Jesus' name. Amen.

(Cf. Ex 13: 21-22)

+++++++

DAILY ACTIVITIES

SHOPPING 1

God of wisdom,
I pray you to guide my shopping,
That I may not over spend,
Or buy things that would sit still in closets and pantries.

Grant me self-control –
In the use of my debit and credit cards.
Let me shop with the principle of the apostle Paul who instructed not to "owe anyone anything except to love".

Help me to be mindful –
That in my manner of shopping,
I would be changing the lives of those for whom I care –
For better or for worse. Amen.

SHOPPING 2

God of all good gifts,
Help me enjoy the beauty of each dress, shirt and trouser,
Of all the fine shoes, bags and accessories,
But hold me back from yielding to temptations,
That would lead to "broke"ness. Amen.

SHOPPING 3

God of health,
Fill my earth-friendly grocery bags with food that will nourish the body - your temple.
And may you cause my palate to agree with the sour, the bitter, and the bland;
That in so doing help me see the good road of years ahead. Amen.

SHOPPING 4

God the provider,
Thank you for providing our needs all the time,
And our wants at times.

We repent of those weak moments when we forget how deep your treasure chest is;
And we keep on hoarding till our faith in you runs dry –
Forgive us and give us grace to trust you unceasingly.

We repent for those greedy moments when we forget to be content with your providence;
And we keep buying more till our spirits are overwhelmed and exhausted –
Forgive us and give us grace to be thankful.

We repent for those selfish moments when we forget to treat the next person in line with respect;
And we push and shove them till we tarnish ourselves - the mirror to reflect your beauty –
Forgive us and give us grace to witness to your name worthily.

In Jesus' name, we pray. Amen.

******

God of the ages,
You provided manna to your hungry children in the desert.

God the Savior of all,
You fed thousands of tired disciples with bread and fish.

God the sustainer,
You continue to nurture and sustain your people eternally.

Make me mindful,
Of the provider that you are that I may find joy in making food for the hungry.
Amen.

******

God our provider,
Help me to take delight in cooking,
That in so doing, I may not only satisfy the physical hunger but nourish the spirit of the hungry.

Amen.

*****

CLEANING I

The trash in the bin,
The dust underneath the bed,
The filth under the carpet,
The stench in the sink,
As I clean them out,
So help me God to look deep
Within my hidden crevices,
And with David pray,
"Search me O God...
See if there is any wicked way in me,"
And make me wholly clean.
Amen.

(Cf., Ps 139: 23-24)

CLEANING 2

God, you are like our mother,
Who works ceaselessly;
Teach us that in doing our household chores,
We serve our family.
In serving our family,
We serve you.

Grant us grace to be as patient as you are;
That even when domestic chores overwhelm us,
We will remember how endlessly your mercy works,
That we, your children, might live well.
Praise be to God! Amen.

CLEANING 3

God, make me a good cleaner of my unclean dishes and souls,
Of dirty floors and minds,
Of soiled laundry and emotions,
Of sticky cobwebs and sin of all kinds.

Let your Holy Spirit be a bar that cleans my soul,
A disinfectant that purifies my mind,
A detergent that removes scars,
And water that makes me white again!
Through Jesus my savior.
Amen.

CLEANING 4

The back aches,
The hands burn,
The eyes are droopy,
The mouth is parched,
The legs are sluggish.

Yet, my Fashioner,
You can strengthen my whole being,
And more –
You can give me joy,
Fill me with peace,
Inspire me to love.

And with your help,
Create a little heaven inside the home!
Through the Holy Spirit, Amen.

******

GARDENING I

The hoes, spades and trowels,
I commit to our care;
Let injuries be ever distant,
And safety be forever near.
Amen.

GARDENING 2

God of all things,
Help me see your purpose in all lives and to be thankful –
For the earthworm which ploughs the soil,
The slugs and snail that fertilize the garden,
The ladybug that eats up insects harmful for plants,
The honey bees that control pests,
The dragonfly that protects us from mosquitoes by feeding on them.
Thank you for your most exquisite creation.
Amen.

GARDENING 3

God who makes all things grow,
Bless the seed sown,
The saplings planted,
The pruning and grafting done,

And as they flourish,
May our hearts rejoice and be thankful to your bounteous favor.
Amen.

******

SOCIAL CONCERNS

God of Creation,
Look at the rivers we have polluted with human wastes and plastics;
Look at the fertile soil we have battered with pesticides and fertilizers;
Look at the firmament we have clouded with fire haze and chemical smoke;
Look at the jungles we have silenced with guns and catapults;
Look at the forests we have shorn off with tools of greed and selfishness;
Look at the environment we have contaminated with foul refuse and manipulative outlook.

Look at the world you created good but have been destroyed by your children.
We have plundered what is yours,
And abused what you've entrusted us with.
We are overwhelmed by disgrace to even seek your mercy,

But without it we will surely perish because of our own doing.
So grant us compassion yet again and restore to us the privilege to care for the earth;
To make them fruitful and plenteous as you ordained from eternity.
For the sake of your beloved Son who makes all things new!
Amen.

(Cf., Gen 1: 28, 31; 2Cor 5: 17)

<<<<<>>>>>

God of beauty,
Thank you for the chirpy sparrows that hop around the rough bushes;
They add beauty and worth to the forgotten plants.

Thank you for the colorful butterflies that dance around the wild flowers;
They call attention to seemingly worthless blossoms.

Thank you for the buzzing bees that twirl around garden blooms;
They sound hope in rejuvenating the earth.

Thank you for the squirrels that scurry up and down that old tree;
They exude energy as to awaken a lethargic world.

Thank you for the cicadas that sing like there's no tomorrow;
They awaken us to live each day to the fullest.

Thank you for the flock of Amur falcons that fly thousands of miles from Africa to roost in Nagaland;
They are reminders of your universal Lordship.

O God, our knowledge of our planet, of you and of ourselves would've been so much poorer;
If not for these priceless creatures you've surrounded us with.

May the name of God the Creator, the Redeemer and the Sustainer be praised!

Amen.

<<<<>>>>

Dear God,
Let the freshness of the air greet me in the morning,
That newness may clothe me everyday.

If the sun should shine today,
May it not scorch the land and burn the fields of those who would go hungry otherwise.

If the wind should blow,
May it not be harsh as to uproot tress and destroy homes of the poor.

If the rain should fall,
May it not take down with it roads and houses that lives maybe lost.

Let the coolness of the breeze bid me welcome in the evening,
That rest may befriend me throughout the night.

And to the ends of the earth, may this prayer pertain. For it is asked in Jesus' name through the divine Spirit.

Amen.

<<<<>>>>

Savior of the universe,
Hear the groaning of every creature and help us.

The indiscriminately felled trees cry out in pain for the world that would perish without them to purify the environment;

The poisoned rivers roar in fear for the world that would cease to survive without them to hydrate it;

The smog-shrouded stars, moon and sun whimper

in sorrow for the world that would linger in darkness without them to give light;

The hunted birds and animals shriek in distress for the world that would no longer be fruitful without them to recreate the forest life.

Redeem our world from madness that leads to the murder of our ecosphere and consequently of each other; that your salvation maybe extended beyond humanity to the tiniest of your creations.

To the worth, praise and honor of you, O God become flesh. Amen.

<<<<>>>>

Righteous God,
Surely your eyes see the sorrow of those poor folks whose lands have been taken away but not compensated.

Surely your ears hear the groaning of those whose jobs have been snatched away from their hands because they have nothing to bribe with.

Surely your heart listens to the yearnings of those who long for shelter, food and clothing instead of lying on cold concrete in an open sky.

Surely your hand is upon those who suffer and upon those who cause suffering alike.

May your righteous indignation be for all to see;
That none may ask, "Where is your God?"

Surely your face is towards those who are landless,
jobless, homeless, cold and hungry.
Come to their rescue and may those who cause them
also see your righteousness revealed and repent.

To the glory of your holy name.
Amen.

::::::::::::::

ONE

God of Grace and Mercy,
Forgive human urge to lord over each other,
Trampling under foot the rights of a neighbor.

ALL

Show us mercy.

ONE

Forgive human greed that steals food from the mouth of the hungry,
Swallowing up their last morsel of dignity.

ALL

Show us mercy

ONE

Forgive human vanity that seeks to forget everyone else except oneself,
Treating all else as a thing to be manipulated for selfish end.

ALL

Show us mercy.

ONE

Forgive human tendency to mistrust one another except for those of our kind,
Regarding 'others' lesser than ourselves.

ALL

Show us mercy.

ONE

Forgive us for despising truth and befriending wickedness,
Only your mercy can make us realize our frailties and constant need of you to resist evil.

ALL

Show us mercy, in the name of Jesus.
Amen.

::::::::::::::

SoLidaRitY Prayer

ONE: Almighty God, the whole world is in the palm of your hands, and the tiniest sparrow does not escape your watchful eyes -
Hold in your hands those at home and outside that are mourning the loss of their rights and freedom;
Their mouths are muted by threats and their feet shackled to a pillar of tyranny.
ALL: Reign among us today.

ONE: Look on those on the streets, fighting against systemic corruption that enfeebles your children to stand morally strong,
Their bodies are shaken by fear and their spirits weary from persistent injustice.
ALL: Reign among us today.

ONE: Hold in your hands those who are silenced by tear gas and injured by water cannon for speaking truth and rallying against evil,
Their righteous fights are disrupted and their commitment trivialized by wanton oppression.
ALL: Reign among us today.

ONE: Look on those who are working for peace in every way possible igniting the light of Christ Jesus in every little corners of the world,
Their passion is marked by mockery and their selfless engagement deemed wasted by rulers walking in darkness.

ALL: Reign among us. Amen.

::::::::::::::

Prophetic Call

God who spoke to ancient prophets,
Speak to our times,
To your people,
The nations,
And to your church.

Speak words of wisdom,
Teach us how sacrifice pales before obedience,
Your indwelling in us transcends churchgoing,
Doing justice pleases you far more than offering of wealth.

Speak judgment to evil ways,
Remind us how you destroyed your people of old for oppressing the poor, crushing the needy, conspiring to steal from the poor,
Warn us how you refuse favor to those who love wickedness and trample on the poor to live in their palatial houses,
They neither eat of their fields and orchards nor reap returns from their fat bank balances.

Speak truth to our hypocrisy,
Let us know how you hate our Christmas celebrations, Passion Week and Easter,
Our routine weekday's fellowship and Sunday worship,
Our music is noise and homily reflects lies,
Impress upon our minds that you desire the change of hearts rather than empty gestures of devotion.

Speak restoration to our broken world,
Help us to believe that in your Son Jesus alone can all things be made new,
And to trust in your promise to make us your people and you our God,
In all things

(Inspired by prophetic books in the Old Testament)

::::::::::::::

Global Intercession

ONE: Almighty God, we gather as one body in your beloved Son, Jesus Christ, through the Holy Spirit to lift our hearts and voices to seek your mercy for the world.

ALL: Be gracious to our petitions.

ONE: We pray for your Church, redeemed by the sacrifice of Jesus Christ for your purpose, that you will continue to embolden her to be salt and light for your glory. Grant the shepherds of all local congregations with all wisdom they need to prepare the flocks under her care to become as holy brides fit and made ready for the return of your Son, the groom. In the life of your people together, let mutual love flourish that your family under Christ may grow in your likeness for your glory. In her task to establish your kingdom and an end to sin and evil, empower her to remain steadfast till the end.

ALL: Be gracious to our petition.

ONE: We pray for the political and civil leaders of the world. Look on your people with love and grant the leaders with the same love with which your loved us and gave your only son. Guide them to paths of righteousness that all their ways and doings may be what you desire the most – to do justice, love kindness and humbly walk with you. And in their so doing, may the loves of the poor, the vulnerable, the rich and the mighty be transformed by your Spirit for your glory and each other's wellbeing.

ALL: Be gracious to our petition.

ONE: We pray for dear and near ones who need healing in their mind, body and spirit. Help those who are going through financial stress and carrying heavy burdens on their weak shoulders. Reconcile unto yourself those searching for meaning in life without the knowledge that you are the fountain of abundant life. Restore relationship amongst the family that in their unity they may find themselves reflecting the perfect communion within the one God in three persons.

ALL: Be gracious to our petition. Amen.

Invocation to the Trinity

Almighty God,
Keep us grounded in your Sovereign Providence.
Bring down the selfish from their egoistic thrones,
And lift up the downtrodden to the height of your gracious glory.

Jesus Immanuel,
Teach us trusting restraint in times of anger.
Humble the powerfuls who repress the needs of the innocent,
Throw open the doors of your kingdom so that the marginalized will sit and feast at your table of salvation.

Spirit Sophia,
Set your children free by your truth.
Many peoples and communities of the world are bound by many untruths,
Break every shackle of falsehood and release those deceived to a life of liberty.

To the Triune God be glory forever.
Amen.

::::::::::::::

ONE: God of the sea, the waves and storm,
The world today is like a sea raging with harsh tempest all around us. Our fragile boats of faith are overwhelmed by its force and we foolishly ask if you are asleep and do not care! Have mercy on our fears and speak peace to us.
ALL: Help us also to say, "Peace! Be still!"

ONE: There are yet other storms of life that destroy homes and nations. Our hearts are saddened by senseless destruction of human lives and possessions due to bombings, airstrikes, gunshots and physical and mental torture. Have mercy on our despair and speak peace to us.
ALL: Help us also to say, "Peace! Be still!"

ONE: Still there are unseen downpours that dampen our spirits. We are tired of powers and principalities that unleash a rule of tyranny whereby the poor suffer discrimination, the orphans rendered hopeless, the widows rejected, the sick stigmatized, and the lonely forgotten. Have mercy on our complacence and speak peace to us.
ALL: Help us also to say, "Peace! Be still!"

ONE: Till every windstorm of life is past and every community on earth is filled with great awe of your universal power, have mercy on our weaknesses and speak peace to us.

ALL: Amen.

(Cf., Mk 4: 35-41)

::::::::::::::

God, whose way is of love,
Glorify your children who are humiliated for the sake of your kingdom virtues.
Forgive those who claim to follow you but only obey evil directions.
Break the hardened hearts of those who refuse your kind disciplining.
Mend our paths till they become paths of love, worthy of your name.
Amen.

PERSONAL PRAYERS

Eternal Life

Creator God,
Now I am young,
My energy is endless;
Life is like a song,
The lyrics are fearless.

Then I'll be old,
My body shall become feeble;
I'll soon see my Lord,
I'll again be made able.

Let neither youth nor age,
Keep me far away;
Or keep me caged,
To eternal decay.
Amen

{{{{{{}}}}}}

The Quiet Spot

Dear Lord
There's a fearful space within;
The fear of the unknown;
The fear of what might be.

That space is hid from sin;
It's where I meet the one who has been known;
And he knows me.

The space is one where I win;
Where the turmoil outside cannot own;
It's that part which is most free.

Shepherd my heart through life's din;
That as the Savior in Gethsemane has shown;
So may faith keep me on my knee.
Amen

{{{{{}}}}}

Only Mercy

Merciful God,
Take my broken heart and make it whole,
Take my shame and my disgrace and make them glorious.
Take my sufferings and make them joyous,
Take my damaged spirit and bring it back to life.
Not that I deserve them,
But because you are compassionate.
Not that I'm entitled to,
But because you allow me to.
Not that I know how to ask,
But because you give to us abundantly and freely, in Jesus' name.
Amen.

{{{{{}}}}}

Master's Hand

My Lord God,
Let me not hunger for people's praise,
Neither despise the critics,
Nor patronize my friends.

In the malice of enemies,
Help me see my strength;
In the flattery of acquaintances,
Help me see my weakness;
In the counsel of godly mentors,
Help me see what I ought to be;
In the gentle rebuke of kith and kin,
Help me see the whole me.
In all things –
Help me see your hand still working on me.
Amen.

{{{{{{}}}}}}

Desires of the Heart

My friend and my God,
I'm an open book wholly known to you.
Turn the pages of my heart,
And attend to its longings.

Forsake not its want of a fit companion,
Neither its need for prosperity,
Nor its yearning for your righteousness.

Awaken it to love with pure intent,
To cheerfully give without expecting returns,
To humbly serve till your reign is real in all communities of the world.

Guide it back to yourself when it transgresses your will,
Shelter it from being part of the world's coldness,
Warm it with your light to bring hope in dark corners.

Make this heart your own,
Fill the empty pages with your pleasures and plans for me,
And teach me to joyfully align mine with yours.

In the name of Jesus, my friend, I pray.
Amen.

{{{{{{}}}}}}

Winning Battles

Faithful God,
My struggle against ______ (name the struggle: alcohol, drugs, gaming, pornography, money, rage, narcissism, etc.) has wearied me,

I'm beaten to the ground;
Unable to stand on my own.

The _______ (name the struggle) has stolen my time,
Defeated my self-esteem,
And plundered my potentials.

I'm a helpless dependent sloth,
Useless before family and community,
A liability wherever I be.

Only your faithfulness can restore me,
Not for any merit of mine,
But only for your name's sake, I turn to you for my mending.

{{{{{{}}}}}}

Alcoholic's Lament

O God of Wisdom,
Look on me with kindness.
The mocker and brawler has led me astray,
I'm a fool!

I'm quick to quarrel,
Slow to reason,
Slower even more to find my way back;
I'm my own enemy!

It has altered my mind,
Ruined valued relationships,
And misplaced priorities;
I'm a mess!

Where can I go to?
Who is my constant help?
What is my destiny?
I'm lost!

O Sophia, send your wisdom,
Impart it on me,
Let it guide me to you and myself;
Then I will be prudent!

My mind shall no longer torment me,
Life shall reap its fullest harvest,
Even to eternity it shall return joyfully;
The steadfast love of the Lord can do it!

{{{{{{}}}}}}

BENEDICTIONS

I

ONE: May the Lord update his will
On the walls of your heart,
And post it for all to see
Your changed status.
And may those to whom you are visible,
Like and share you to others –
For the glory of God.
ALL: Amen.

(Inspired by Facebook)

II

ONE: Disperse now from the house of God into the world to do what the Lord requires of you –
To do justice, and to love kindness, and to walk humbly with your God.
And may the Triune God be eternally glorified.
ALL: Amen.

(Adapted from Micah 6: 8)

III

ONE: May you leave well,
May you stay well,
May your news be good,
In the power of the Triune God.
All: Amen.

IV

ONE: May the blessings of God be as refreshing as the dews on the tree,
May they be as plenty as the flock of birds in the sky,
May they be as constant as the flowing of water in the river.
ALL: Amen.

V

ONE: The Lord God walk with you through every valley of darkness; and bring you light.
The Lord God stand by you at every height

of despair; and bring you joy.
The Lord God sit beside you in every moment of weakness; and bring you deliverance.

ALL: Amen.

VI

May your feet not stumble against any stone of temptation,

May your hands not be soiled by any dirt of sin,

May your feet not tread any path of wickedness,

That God's holy name maybe known to every nation.
Amen.

VII

Stay ever in the presence of God, understanding as he speaks, listening as he instructs, following as he leads, and resting as he fights your battles; to him be glory forever. Amen.

VIII

Go out into the world, Oh people of God,

To speak well of each other,

To uplift the downtrodden,

To speak life into dry spirits,

And in so doing to proclaim the Gospel of Christ till his return in glory.

Amen

IX

God, may the boldness of your Spirit transform us,

May the Goodness of your Spirit guide us,

May the gift of your Spirit prepare us as we go out into the world in the name of Jesus Christ.

Amen